Scrum

Your Quick Start Guide To Adopting Scrum For Your Organization

By Jefferson Hanley

Legal Notice:

This ebook is copyright protected. This is only for personal use. You cannot amend, distribute, sell, use, quote or paraphrase any part or the content within this ebook without the consent of the author or copyright owner. Legal action will be pursued if this is breached.

Disclaimer Notice:

Please note the information contained within this document is for educational purposes only.

Every attempt has been made to provide accurate, up to date and reliable complete information no warranties of any kind are expressed or implied. Readers acknowledge that the author is not engaging in rendering legal, financial or professional advice.

By reading any document, the reader agrees that under no circumstances are we responsible for any losses, direct or indirect, which are incurred as a result of use of the information contained within this document, including – but not limited to errors, omissions, or inaccuracies.

Table of Contents

PREAMBLE

The inspiration for this book came out of my desire to tell people about Scrum, and to encourage individuals and groups to adopt this unbelievable methodology for projects across their organizations. What I have tried to do in this book, is provide you a snapshot of Scrum in the hope that you will be encouraged by its simplicity. Hopefully, once you realize what power Scrum holds, and how simple it is to adopt, you will embrace it, even with little or no formal training.

OBJECTIVES OF THIS BOOK

The body of Scrum knowledge is indeed like a vast, deep mighty ocean. No single publication can claim to simplify all of that knowledge, in its entirety. Neither does this book!

Instead, the objective of this book is to deliver readers a quick preview of the main principles of Scrum, and then provide you with some practical advice on how to get started with adopting those principles in a real-world project setting. By the time you have completed reading this book, you will understand:

- Why project management methodologies are important

- What differentiates Scrum from traditional methodologies like Waterfall
- The Scrum Framework
- How work is carried out by a Scrum Team within the Scrum Framework
- What to do in order to put Scrum in action in your organization
- What practical measures to adopt to succeed in Scrum projects
- What benefits Scrum can deliver across your organization
- What scrum training options are available to you

Happy reading!

1.0 INTRODUCTION

1.1 Why Use Project Management Methodologies

For those of you that are new to the science (and some

> **Good to know:**
>
> *An individual or collaborative enterprise that is carefully planned to achieve a particular aim.*

would argue the art!) of Project Management, a "Project" has a very specific definition. According to the Project Management Institute, a project comprises of a set of temporary activities designed to produce a specific result. To qualify as a "project", these activities must be conducted within a defined start and end timeframe. By definition therefore, any planned activity - say, for example, doing a grocery run - could qualify as a "project", provided it meets the aforementioned criteria. In the case of our grocery run, one may need (at minimum) to have a predefined grocery list handy, and then plan their buying in a way that's efficient and avoids issues (missing items, or buying more than one planned!).

But as the activity gets more complex - say, for example, building an aeroplane - one must embrace a higher degree of discipline to ensure a successful outcome. The more complex the project gets, the greater the need to follow tried and tested methodologies to:

- Initiate
- Plan
- Execute
- Monitor
- Control, and
- Close out

the project.

A project management methodology is therefore nothing but a set of proven guidelines that will help Project Managers to finish their projects on-time, on-spec and within budget. Using a formal methodology is what gives PM's the ability to deliver success. The alternate to not using a well-defined PM methodology is unacceptable - it's chaos and guaranteed failure!

1.2 Introducing The Two Cousins: Waterfall & Agile

Two commonly well regarded PM methodologies are:

- Waterfall and
- Agile

Both of these methodologies have been extensively used in project management environments, including for software engineering projects. While this book will focus extensively on an Agile methodology, Scrum, it behoves us to take a closer look under the hood of these two cousins first.

1.2.1 Waterfall

The Waterfall methodology dates back to the end of World War II, and owe its origins to managing large-scale manufacturing projects for the defence industry. The core methodology is process driven, and provides Project Managers a framework of phases through which a project must go through before a project is considered complete.

Waterfall phases include:

- Requirement definition
- Design

- Development
- Testing
- Deployment

A hallmark of Waterfall is that is it a sequence-based methodology, in that the project cannot proceed to Design phase unless the Requirement definition phase has been successfully signed off.

1.2.2 Agile

Early experimentation with an alternate PM methodology, known as Agile, took place in the 1990's. While Waterfall stipulated a set of phases, Agile methodologies prescribe a set of interactions and guidelines that project managers adapt to their unique project needs.

Good to know:

Individuals and interactions over processes and tools

Working software over comprehensive documentation

Customer collaboration over contract negotiation

Responding to change over following a plan.

Extracts from The Agile Manifesto

The hallmark of Agile methodologies, of which Scrum is one, is that they rely on a set of iterative cycles to complete projects in small sets of deliverables. Agile places a high degree of emphasis on self-managed teams, without enforcing rigid "project management".

The end result is a rather flexible approach to defining project requirements, and then delivering projects in accordance to the needs of clients.

1.2.3 Same Yet Different!

While both Waterfall and Agile are "proven" methodologies in their own right, both have had their fair share of proponents and opponents. In defence of both advocates and dissuaders of these methodologies, there are as many successful projects as there are failures using either methodology.

The table below summarizes the similarities and differences between the two methodologies:

Feature	Waterfall	Agile
Focus	Typically project-centric focus	Usually product-focused

Management style	Manages specialist activities	Manages product functionality/features produced by entire teams
Planning	Produces a Master Plan up front at inception of project	Uses smaller, self-contained Time-Boxed plans using JIT (Just-In-Time) approach
Deliverables	Can be Waterfall or incremental (iterative) based	All deliverables are incremental (iterative) based
Teams	Usually manages top-down team structures	Are always self-managed

While Waterfall follows more of an "adaptive" approach, in that it defines a set of distinct "phases" that you adapt into your project; Agile is more of a "prescriptive" methodology, in that it prescribes "rules" that can be then adapted by the project manager (note the use of non-capitalized "p" and "m").

Another distinction between the two is in how team roles and interactions are defined. Waterfall teams have much more "rigid" hierarchical boundaries around their roles, while Agile teams are more flexible in their roles.

Additionally, the focus of the Waterfall approach is to deliver a "final product" at the end of the project, while Agile methodologies believe in providing "usable product" throughout the project life, albeit in small increments. For Waterfall projects, the litmus test of a product (or service) can't be conducted until all components are delivered at the end of the project. If there are significant shortfalls, it's back to the drawing board!

This last "peculiarity" of Waterfall is now causing Project Management professionals to look more favourably at Agile as a viable methodology that addresses the issue of when "working solutions" should be delivered by projects.

The concept of "Fail Quickly", which is espoused by Agile, states that by delivering projects in gradual increments, one can find out much earlier in the project timeline if something won't work. If there's an issue, you discover it quickly and can quickly fix it.

Being nimble about quickly fixing the issues and delivering a "usable" version, before moving on to building the next component, is at the heart of what Agile methodologies like Scrum are all about.

2.0 SCRUM

2.1 The Agile Framework

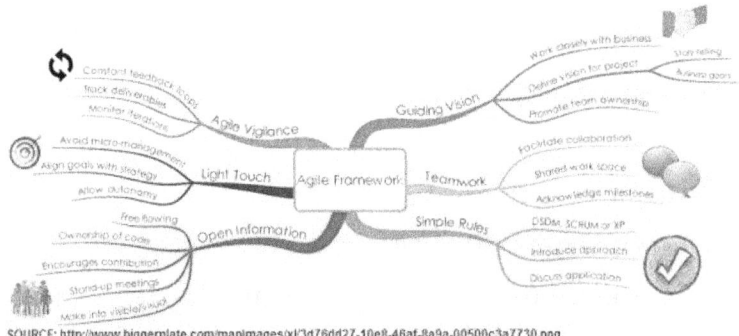

In order to be an effective tool for its adherents, any body of knowledge needs a formal framework within which to function. Agile is no exception. Agile methodologies like Scrum {and others, like Dynamic System Development Methodology (DSDM) or Extreme Programming (XP)}, work within a framework that governs how the various tenants of the Agile body of knowledge should be applied to project management.

Unlike Waterfall, which stipulates that the project be run as distinct phases, with deliverables (either final or interim) being produced at the end of the project, Agile instead prescribes a set of conventions that project managers can then adapt when delivering projects. Hallmarks of the Agile Framework include:

- **Agile Vigilance:** Which stresses the need to build feedback loops within the project that continually monitor and track all aspects of the project, and to adapt themselves to the project's dynamic environment

- **Light Touch:** Which encourages a much higher degree of project team autonomy than Waterfall does. Project teams move away from an environment of strictly imposed order, and gravitate into self-managed structures
- **Open Information:** This enables the free flow of information and views between all stakeholders on the project. This allows the team to assess changing conditions and quickly adapt their responses accordingly
- **Guiding Vision:** The objective here is to facilitate behavioural changes that ultimately result in internal and external stakeholders working to achieve a common goal. The vision is shared by everyone, and so it influences positive outcomes, which leads to project success
- **Collaboration & Teamwork:** This part of the framework is meant to promote healthy interactions between teams, and encourage cooperation amongst everyone in order to meet the desired goals
- **Simple Rules:** The Agile Framework recognizes that a simple set of guiding principles (rules) can often be used to support extremely complex environments, including interactions and relationships amongst team members. The more

complex these rules get, the greater chances of misunderstandings that lead to project failure

Using this framework, Agile methodologies like Scrum are able to manage projects that function in dynamically changing environments, and which can respond quickly to the changing functional demands of their stakeholders.

2.2 What Is Scrum?

Literally speaking, the word "Scrum" is an adaption of the work "scrummage", and denotes a situation of confusion and chaos. The term "Scrum" has its roots in the sports world.

Good to know:

A rugby scrum restarts a rugby game after a minor infringement of the rules. Understand what goes on. Who puts in? How do you win?

Definition of a "Scrum" - Rugby Sidestep

If you are a Rugby fan, you'll often witness scenes like that depicted by the picture here. That, essentially, is what a scrum looks like out on the Rugby field.

Readers of a book on Project Management might well ask "So, what's Rugby got to do with the project management methodology"? Lot's actually, since the methodology owes its origins to the Rugby playing

SOURCE: http://blogs.independent.co.uk/wp-content/uploads/2011/03/scrum1.jpg

fields. That concept of Rugby players "Scrumming" and

regrouping to start off an interruption in play, has been taken and adapted by project management experts, and applied to the world of managing projects.

2.2.1 Scrum In The Project World

In order to win, sports teams need to be nimble, just as project teams must be agile to be successful. When we look at how "typical" projects work, we see striking similarities to the sports world. Individuals (Players) form groups (Teams) and work on specific tasks (Plays) to deliver successfully (Win) on commitments made to stakeholders (Fans). Periodically, there are frictions (Infringements) amongst individuals and groups, and project members have to

> **Good to know:**
>
> *A Scrum is a way for teams to work together to develop a product. Product development, using Scrum, occurs in small pieces, with each piece building upon previously created pieces. Building products one small piece at a time encourages creativity and enables teams to respond to feedback and change, to build exactly and only what is needed.*
>
> Definition of "agile" Scrum - Scrum.org

regroup (Scrummage) to sort things out.

Management experts took all of those similarities, wrapped them around a proven body of project management knowledge, and created an agile approach to managing and delivering projects, which they called "Scrum".

In developing the Scrum methodology, experts realized that there needed to be a certain discipline behind the science of project management. What they discovered is that projects can consistently be delivered to spec, on time and within budget, if PMs:

- Organize the business into smaller self-governing, cross-functional teams;
- Organize work into smaller chunks of deliverables;
- Rank, prioritize and estimate completion and delivery;
- Organize delivery of small "working components" into shorter fixed-timeframe (1 to 4 week) Iterations (or "Sprints")
- Consult with customers/end users and organize release plans based on inspection results of each iteration
- Optimize the entire process based on retrospective review following every iteration

This is the central idea from which Scrum evolved.

2.3 The Scrum Framework

Delivering a project in accordance with the requirements of various stakeholders is an inherently challenging task. However, Scrum has made that challenge easier to navigate by prescribing a "framework" for conducting the project management process.

The Scrum framework revolves around some basic "Scrum values" that practitioners must adhere to, including:

- Commitment

- Openness
- Focus
- Courage and
- Respect

Within these value parameters, complex projects can be delivered through collaboration and effective teamwork. The main focus of successful Scrum is to try and effectively manage a Product Backlog of deliverables that represent the "whole". This, in turn, is done by breaking up the "whole" into smaller deliverable backlogs known as Sprint Backlog. As each Sprint is completed, it adds value to the deliverables produced by previous Sprints, so that the final Sprint marks the culmination of the project.

Scrum Framework

24 Hours

Product Backlog — Sprint Backlog — 2-4 Weeks

Potentially shipable Product Increment

SOURCE: http://www.expertprogrammanagement.com/wp-content/uploads/2010/08/scrum-framework-diagram.jpg

Within this framework, Scrum uses Scrum Teams that are governed by predetermined Roles, Events, Artifacts, and Rules.

2.3.1 Scrum Teams

In the real world, Scrum Teams are a collective name given to several sets of roles that are performed by individuals and groups working on a Scrum driven project. The key to a successful Scrum project is to ensure that you put the right team in place, and that everyone on the team:

- Agrees to pursue common goals
- Embraces a common set of rules and norms
- Respects each and every member on the team
- Values all input given by every member

Without these prerequisites in place, a Scrum project is doomed to failure from the outset.

While many novice PMs think of Scrum (Agile) teams in the context of "hitting the ground running", the truth is that because of their cross-functional nature, that might often not be the case. Veteran Scrum PMs will, however, always build flexibility in their plans for the Forming, Storming, Norming, Performing and Adjourning cycles (as defined by the Tuckman model, and adapted subsequently - more on this later!) to play out before the team gets down to productive business.

Scrum teams are, by definition, cross-functional in their setup. That means you will likely have people on the team with diverse skill sets, many of who have never worked together (as a coherent team), and some that will probably be part of a team for a very short duration, and then be replaced by others.

2.3.2 Scrum Roles

It is in this context therefore that the Scrum Team must be organized around specific team roles.

2.3.2.1 Scrum Master:

This role ensures that the Team follows Scrum best practices, and adheres to the Norms and Rules that the team agrees to follow. Typically, this role is one of a:

- Protector (who shields the team from external disruptions)
- Coach
- Facilitator
- Moderator
- Cheer Leader

At project initiation, the Scrum Master is usually unable to directly contribute to actual Sprint goals. His/her main goal will be to shape the team, and to get them to focus on delivering on committed goals. However, with the passage of time, as the team settles into the "performing" stage, the Scrum Master could potentially start doing "real" work.

Ideally, the Scrum Master should have the confidence of all team members, and must not have any conflict of interest (real or perceived), when it comes to his/her relationship with any of the team members.

2.3.2.2 Product Owner:

This is a combination of the role performed by the traditional "Product manager" and "Project manager". The Product Owner acts as the go between to the Scrum Team and other stakeholders, and is responsible for making sure that the Team is working on the right deliverables at the right time.

In addition to working closely with the Scrum Team on other agreed roles, the Product Owner primarily:

- Manages the Scrum Product Backlog
- Decides what deliverables must be produced, and when
- Controls the Release Schedule of the completed deliverables
- Seeks any clarifications (from external sources) for the Scrum Team about Product Backlog Items (PBIs)

Communication, between the Scrum Team and diverse groups of stakeholders, is a primary role of the Product Owners. The role should therefore be filled by someone with strong written and verbal communication skills. Additionally, to perform this role, requires someone with good negotiation and stakeholder management skills.

2.3.2.3 The Team:

In addition to what has been said earlier about Scrum Teams in general, these teams have certain other characteristics that set them apart from teams using other project management methodologies (like Waterfall). The core Scrum Team:

- Is often relatively small, usually between 5 to 8 individuals. Additional Subject Matter Experts (SMEs) can be called upon as needed
- Does not have sub-teams - it functions as an entity unto itself
- Works with great degree of autonomy as a self-organized unit
- Is very much self-governed, taking their direction from within the team and the Rules and Norms they have agreed to adopt
- Works best when staffed with full-time resources
- Should preferably be collocated

As a group, the team is responsible for:

- Producing and maintaining certain Scrum artifacts (more on this later), primarily the Sprint Backlog
- Organizing, running and participating in the Daily Sprint Meeting
- Working collectively to produce a shippable deliverable at the end of each Sprint

- Ensuring that status updates to team dashboards, specifically the Sprint Burn down Chart, are regular and accurate

2.3.3 Scrum Events

Scrum projects are carried out through a series of events, which are geared towards producing all of the project deliverables. Additionally, there are other Scrum Events which serve to manage timelines and quality of the deliverables, as well as conduct self-appraisals of the overall Scrum (and Sprint) processes that were followed, and adopt measures to streamline them where necessary.

2.3.3.1 The Sprint:

Within the Scrum Framework, all project activities designed to deliver items in the Scrum Product Backlog are performed via an event known as the Sprint (or "Iteration"). Sprints are usually confined to time-boxed durations of between 1 and 4 weeks.

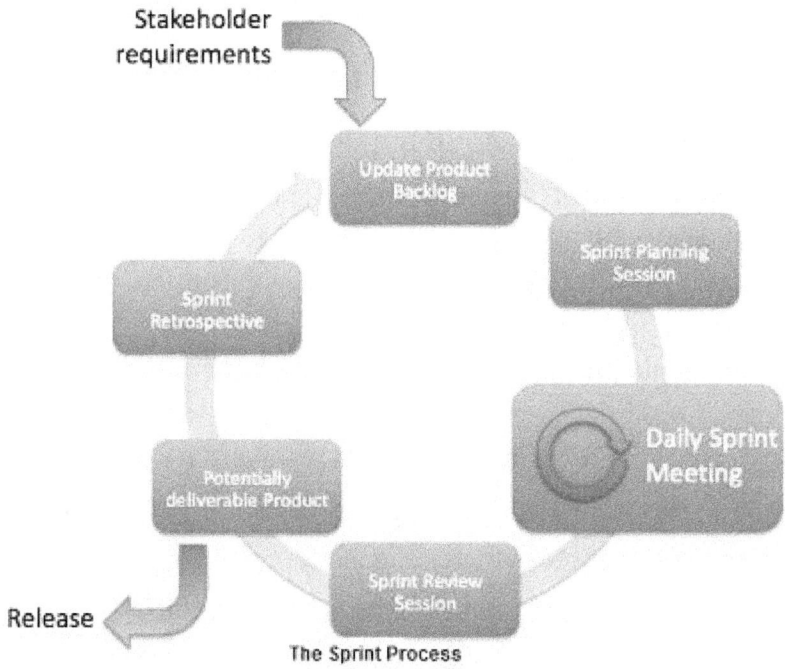

The Sprint Process

SOURCE: Scrum-Institute.Org

The objective of the sprint is to create the ideal conditions so that the project team "sprints" to finish all of the deliverables that are on the Sprint Backlog.

2.3.3.2 Sprint Planning:

Each Sprint commences with two sets of planning sessions - a WHAT and a HOW. In the WHAT session, the Scrum Team reviews the Product Backlog and agrees upon what items from there will be delivered in the current Sprint.

Team members are allowed to freely express their views on whether the commitments can be met, or if they see potential hurdles in delivery. Once the team has agreed upon what is to be included in the current Sprint, they commence discussing HOW to deliver on the WHAT.

The HOW session takes all of the WHAT deliverables and breaks them down into specific tasks, estimates timelines for them, and assigns responsibilities for each task to individuals (or groups) on the project team.

2.3.3.3 Daily Scrum Meetings:

Now that the Scrum Team has received it's "marching orders" for what needs to be delivered by the end of the Sprint (in 1 to 4 weeks time), the team meets daily to manage its workload and ensure progress is being made.

The Scrum Master facilitates the Daily Scrum Meetings, and participation of all team members is mandatory. These meetings are "stand up" sessions, and should be no more than 15-minutes in duration. If there are significant items flagged during the session, they should not be ignored due to lack of time. "Off line" meetings could be scheduled to deal with such items separately.

During the Daily Scrum Meeting (also called the Daily Stand Up Meeting), the Scrum Master will review the following with each team member:

- What was accomplished by him/her since the previous Daily Scrum Meeting?
- What prevented him/her from meeting their goals?

- What do they plan on accomplishing prior to the next session?

The Sprint Backlog is updated as a result of these daily sessions to reflect the current status of the Sprint.

2.3.3.4 The Sprint Review:

Since each Sprint is meant to culminate with completion of certain deliverables, this implies that the Sprint Review will be held once those deliverables have, in fact, been completed.

During these sessions, held at the end of a Sprint, the Scrum Team demonstrates all of the Sprint Backlog items completed. The Product Owner is responsible for accepting (in line with predetermined acceptance criteria) or rejecting any Sprint Backlog item. Should an item be rejected, the Product Owner will remove it from the Sprint Backlog and add it (back) to the Product Backlog. Such items are then reviewed and reprioritized for possible inclusion in subsequent Sprints.

The Sprint Review should be kept as informal as possible, with less emphasis on ceremony and more on substance - such as decisions indicating status of Sprint Backlog items: "accepted", "rejected", "needs some improvement".

2.3.3.4 The Sprint Retrospective:

As its name implies, this is a retrospective look at the recently completed Sprint. The Sprint Retrospective meeting should be conducted immediately following the completion of a Sprint, and must focus on the following three things:

- What the Scrum Team did well during the Sprint?
- What didn't go as planned during the Sprint?
- What improvements need to be made so things can go even better in the next Sprint?

The Scrum Master facilitates these sessions, and it is mandatory for the entire Scrum Team to attend and provide feedback. The Scrum Master documents these sessions and updates the Scrum "lessons learned" and best practices documentation for future reference.

2.3.4 Scrum Artifacts

Like any good process or methodology, Scrum prescribes certain tools, called Scrum Artifacts, which help practitioners document the overall project. The Scrum Team and other stakeholders also use these artifacts as visual aids to manage and keep track of progress being made on the project as well as individual Sprints (Iterations).

2.3.4.1 Product Backlog:

All project teams, regardless of the methodology they follow to manage the project, need some kind of "list of features" to work towards. In its simplest form, the Scrum Product Backlog may be considered as the entire universe of features (User Stories) that must be delivered in order to consider the project completed.

It is important to note that the Product Backlog goes well beyond a simple "To Do" list. This tool ranks and prioritizes all of the features of the product that are in scope for the project. More importantly, it provides a link back to the specific Use Cases (User Stories), as well as to the particular Sprint in which the feature will be (or has been) delivered.

The Product Backlog serves as an important artifact during the Sprint Planning Meeting, as it is used to identify which features (User Stories) should be included in the forthcoming Sprint. Team members then assess each item and decide if they can deliver it, or propose alternate prioritization (e.g. including it in the Sprint after the forthcoming one).

The Product Owner owns and maintains the Product Backlog, and uses it to track progress of deliverables within each Sprint. However, the Scrum Master and Scrum Team also contribute to providing updates to the Product Backlog.

	Priority	ID	Component	Story Points	In Sprint
Not new	1	6	X	3	✖
	2	14	X	2	✔
	3	18	X	2	✖
	4	19	U	2	✔
New	5	21	Y	1	✔
	6	22	X	2	✖
	7	23	Z	3	✔
	8	24	U	2	✖
	9	25	V	1	✔
	10	26	X	3	✖
	11	27	U	2	✖
	12	28	Z	1	✔
	13	29	Z	2	✔
	14	30	V	1	✔
	15	31	V	3	✖

SOURCE: Scrum Alliance.Org

2.3.4.2 Sprint Backlog:

Once specific Product Backlog Items (PBIs) are selected for inclusion in a Sprint, the challenge is to monitor and track all of the tasks needed to deliver those PBI during the Sprint. The Sprint Backlog is yet another powerful tool that helps Scrum Teams stay on top of what needs to be done to accomplish their goals.

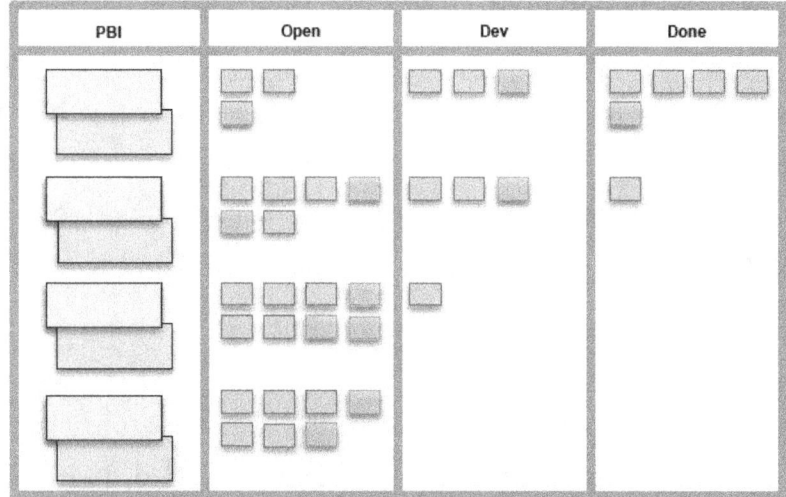

The Sprint Task Board

The Sprint Backlog provides a visual picture of:

- The PBI (or User Stories) that are scheduled for delivery during the current Sprint
- The list of open tasks that must be completed in order for each PBI to be considered "done"
- A subset of those "open" tasks that have been assigned to a developer and are actively being worked upon
- A list of development tasks that have been completed ("done")

When a team member is assigned a task, the task is removed from the "Open" queue and entered in the "Dev" queue, with his/her name against it. As and when a task is finished, it is removed from "Dev" and added to the "Done" queue.

Scrum Teams own and manage the Sprint Backlog, and it is updated daily (often several times a day). It is reviewed during the Daily Stand-up meeting, and updates made for everyone to see. Usually, it is helpful for the team to also estimate "time to complete" and "time left to finish" in person-hours so that all team members and stakeholders have a clear indication of work in progress and effort remaining.

2.3.4.3 Burn Down Chart:

Managing projects requires keeping a keen eye on what's happening, in terms of how work is being finished, and what is expected to happen, in terms of forecasting future outcomes. The Burn Down Chart is an excellent tool in the arsenal of the Agile PM to accomplish both those objectives.

This tool helps PMs and other stakeholders see exactly how quickly the Scrum Team is "burning" through the Product Backlog (User Stories). The Burn Down chart:

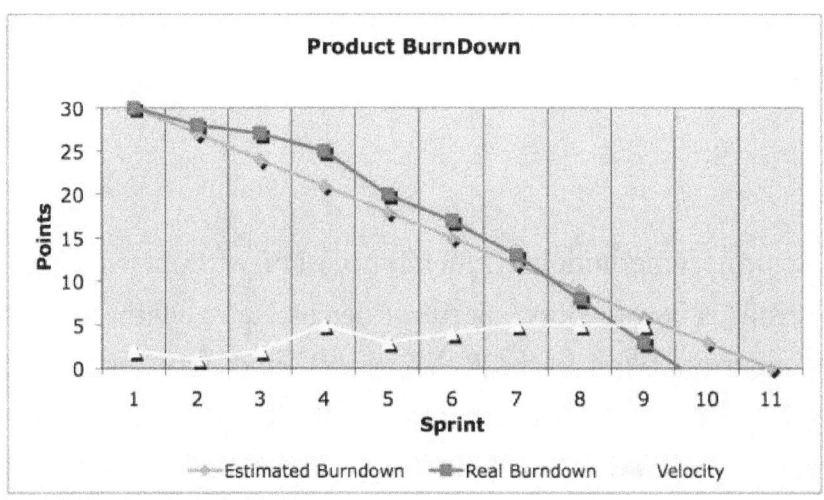

SOURCE: http://www.scrum-institute.org/

- Is a visual aid that helps show progress made on completing various milestones to deliver the final product
- It compares how the team is doing (Real Burn Down), in terms of effort in finishing deliverables
- It projects what completion will look like (Estimated Burn Down) if the current rate of progress is maintained
- Plots the progress rate (Velocity) of the Scrum Team

PMs can use various formats of Burn Down Charts to focus on various metrics, such as "Total Effort versus Work Done"; "Total Effort versus Work Remaining"; "Effort versus Velocity". These views will help the Scrum Master and Product Owner decide how to manage slippage (if any), or reprioritize PBIs in a more realistic way.

The Burn Down Charts should be reviewed during each Daily Scrum Meeting, and Team Members should be allowed to comment on why things aren't progressing as planned (e.g. due to many new requests added to the Sprint Backlog mid-Sprint!).

2.3.4 Scrum Rules

No project methodology can be successful without rules, and Scrum is no exception. Scrum rules are the glue that binds the Scrum Team to the Roles, Events and Artifacts within the overall Scrum Framework. While some methodologies have extremely rigid rules that govern them, what sets Scrum rules apart is that they are more inclusive and flexible in nature.

While some of these rules are guidelines for adopting Scrum best practices, others take the form of general norms that should be encouraged within a project setting. Together, these rules and norms will then govern the interaction between team members and stakeholders.

Here are some key Scrum Rules that Scrum practitioners must be aware of:

- Sprint lengths should be of the same duration
- No Sprint should exceed 4 weeks in length
- Teams shall not take inter-Sprint breaks (Sprints must follow a continuous, unbroken cycle)
- Everyone on the team must understand that the end objective of a Sprint is to create a "potentially shippable" product
- Each Sprint must start with a Sprint Planning meeting

- Sprint Planning meetings must be timeboxed (2 to 3 hours)
- Each day of the Sprint must begin with a Daily Scrum meeting
- The Daily meetings should be timeboxed (15 minutes at the most)
- All team members must attend the Daily meeting
- The date, time and location of every meeting should be publicised
- Each Sprint must be concluded with a Sprint Review meeting
- Each Sprint Review meeting should then be followed by a Sprint Retrospective, which all team members must attend
- When prioritizing Product Backlog Items (PBIs or User Stories), no two items can have the same priority
- If there are any known defects in the previous Sprint (Iteration), those must be prioritized for resolution at the highest level in the upcoming Sprint
- Team meetings must be open and fair, with all members (and stakeholders) allowed to express their points of views
- Scrum Teams (Scrum Master, Product Owner and Scrum Team members) are encouraged to use prominently positioned visual displays (Backlogs) to highlight progress

- When a team member is facing a challenge delivering his/her commitments, he/she shall actively seek out assistance from others who are able to support him/her
- Scrum Team members who complete their assignments ahead of time must actively volunteer for additional tasks from the "Open" list

While rules will certainly help bring order and discipline within project teams, no amount of rules can actually prevent chaos - unless everyone on the team abides by the rules. The key principles behind Scrum Rules therefore are:

- Everyone must be consulted before a rule is proposed
- All Team members and stakeholders must agree to abide by the rules
- The rules must be well publicised
- There should be consequences for not following a rule

Ultimately, these rules and norms are high-level guidelines for PMs to refer to when managing their projects. Common sense should be used when adopting them, and they should be tailored to adapt to a specific project's needs, if required.

3.0 SCRUM IN ACTION

Now that we have a good understanding of the Scrum Framework, and comprehend the importance of Scrum Teams, it's time to consider what it takes to put these principles into action in the real world. It matters not how well one is trained in various Scrum disciplines, and it won't count if you have all the knowledge about project management on your side. Unless you are prepared to be flexible in your approach, you won't get too far implementing Scrum in real world project settings.

3.1 Building the Team

At the heart of a successful Scrum project is a successful team. And the success of the team itself is not in what individual contributors are able to do, but in what the team is collectively able to deliver. And there lies the challenge for

Scrum practitioners. One may have the best and brightest individuals assigned to a project, but if they don't (or are not able to) work together towards a common goal, their brilliance will mean nothing to the project.

And that gives rise to yet another team challenge: Given that Scrum teams are devoid of any formal and specific "project manager" role, how does one actually manage to get a team of individuals, some of whom may never have worked together before, to successfully deliver all of the Product Backlog Items? And the answer is: By using a bit of human psychology, and some cunning and craft.

3.1.1 The Individual's Mindset

In the real world, individuals who are Scrum project team members are unlikely to respond to some of the stimuli that might motivate individuals in the general workforce. Ideals like "job security" and "promotions" are not something that will drive a Scrum Team member to give his/her best to the team. To build effective Scrum Teams therefore, we need to look into the mindset of potential team members.

Way back in 1954 Abraham Maslow, the "Father of humanistic psychology", came up with a pyramid that depicted a hierarchy of human needs. According to Maslow, individuals have 5 sets of distinct needs that must be satisfied. Maslow's findings are important to us today, because somewhere along that pyramid we will find what motivates individuals on a Scrum Team. And if we wish to build effective teams, then we must understand the mind set of potential Scrum Team members.

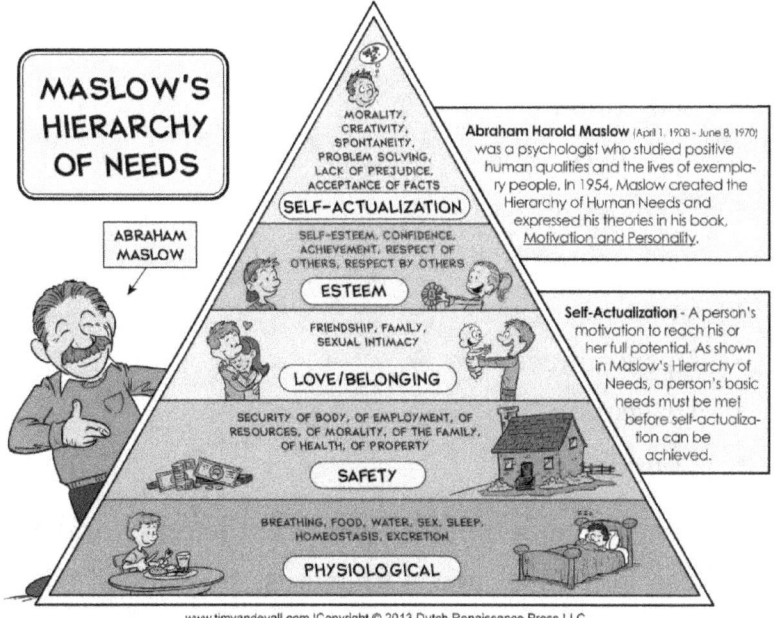

Maslow theorized that Physiological needs, such as food, water and other bodily needs formed the bottom of the Human Needs pyramid.

Next come Safety needs, which in the context of a project team member might equate to job security, security of income, owning a home and prospering from decent employment.

Then, next in line came Love and Belonging needs, which speak to an individual's need for social relationships.

The last two types of needs, Self Esteem and Self-actualization are what should interest Scrum practitioners the most, because that's what will drive Scrum Team members the most. These are the human needs that determine feelings like:

- Self-fulfilment
- Self-content
- Self-motivation
- Confidence
- Peer respect
- Creativity
- Open-mindedness
- Dedication
- Commitment

If you want to put Scrum into action in the real world, then it is those individual needs that must be fulfilled so that Scrum Team members can contribute to the projects' goals.

3.1.2 Creating and "Managing" The Team

So, given that Maslow's assessment of human needs theory is accurate (and it is, because it has stood the test of time!), then how does one go about choosing individuals to build a successful Scrum Team?

Here are a few practical suggestions for building the team and making it function effectively:

- Scrum Teams draw strength from collective performance. That means, even if he/she is a strong contributor individually, if a team member is unable to function in a group setting, his/her inclusion in the Scrum Team could be potentially disruptive

- When selecting team members, be sure to ensure that they can be genuine contributors. Individuals that have no value-add to offer will only be a drag on the team's efficiency

- As an extension to the point above, Scrum Teams must be built with breadth of expertise rather than depth. Scrum Teams are cross-functional groups. Having 3 Business Analysts or 4 Structural Engineers with the same experience profile on the team won't work. Identify as many unique skill sets required to deliver all of the PBI for the project, then go about selecting your team

- This leads us directly to our next suggestion - team size. Too small teams can lead to individuals carrying too much burden, and therefore burning out quickly. And too large a team size can lead to inefficiencies. Most modern day Management Scientists agree that the optimal span of management is between 5 to 8 individuals. A team size larger than that will mean:
  - Many more points of friction amongst team members
  - The need for even more "management" interactions between Scrum Master, Product Owner and Team members
  - Greater coordination and communication overhead

It is to avoid all of these distractions that Scrum teams are recommended to be smaller in size compared to teams in other methodologies like Waterfall

- Once again, staying on the team size discussion, while the core team size should be kept manageable, there is no harm in adding temporary members to balance the team's skill set. A good practice is identifying additional Subject Matter Experts (SMEs) from across the organization, and having them contribute on an as-and-when needed basis. This "identification" process must begin early on in the project lifecycle, and the individual SME's must be notified of their potential roles as soon as possible

- One hallmark of Scrum Teams is the fact they are lead without the use of formal "authority". When "managing" Scrum Teams therefore, it's never a good idea to say "This is what I want you to do. Now go do it!" Use Maslow's Self-Actualization formula to get team members to brainstorm and come up with actionable ideas themselves. That approach goes a long way to making Scrum Teams feel empowered

- In a previous section of this book we discussed the idea of Rules and Norms. As we discuss the practical implications of putting Scrum in action, it is worth stressing the need for those Rules and Norms once again. Team success can only be assured if everyone knows the rules, and everyone agrees to follow them

- Just as clarity of team rules and norms is important, so too is clarity of purpose and objectives. The Daily Scrum Meetings should be used as a forum for reiterating the purpose and objectives the team has before them. The more they hear about it, the more driven they will be to accomplish those goals

3.1.3 Team Dynamics

As someone who is responsible for forming a Scrum Team, you must also be aware of some famous management theories governing team dynamics. The most famous of these is the Tuckman model (referred to earlier in this book), which simply stated can be interpreted as: "Teams don't just 'hit the ground running'...they need time to form themselves".

While Scrum projects are characterized by their agility and fast turnaround of deliverables, the formation time of the Scrum Team (especially if this is the first time the team is working together as a unit) will need to be factored into the equation.

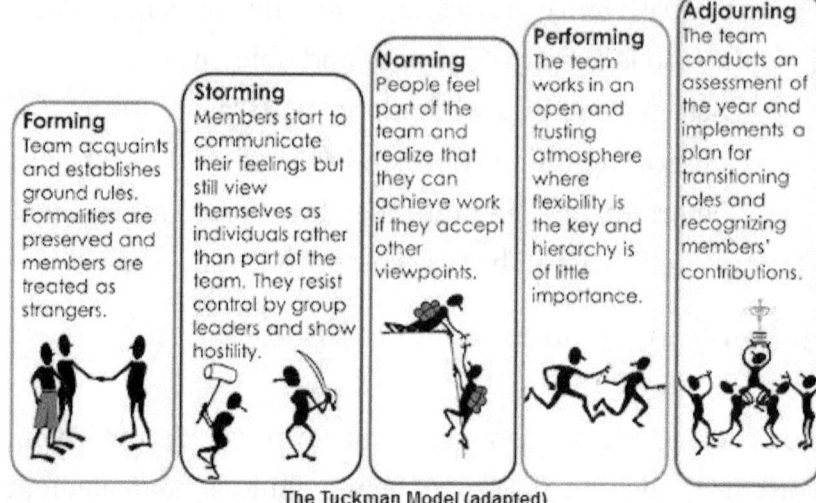

The Tuckman Model (adapted)

The Forming, Storming, Norming, Performing and Adjourning stages must be allowed to play out if the team is to deliver its best over the project's life.

Scrum Masters will need to play a big role in encouraging healthy team dynamics. It might therefore help if the Scrum Master has some background (or experience) in coaching and counseling. Negotiating with individuals and getting their buy-in is what works for Scrum Team members, not commanding or directing!

3.2 Successful Scrum Tips

So far we have seen that embracing Scrum in a project setting is really no big deal. All it really requires is a common sense approach to:

- Identifying what needs to be done

- Organizing a team to do it
- Ensuring the team delivers as planned

Well, Scrum practitioners who have seen Scrum in action will tell you that all of this is easier said than done! However, those same practitioners will also attest to the fact that it is possible to run successful projects using the Scrum methodology. Here are some practical tips that veteran Scrum professionals give to novices:

- **Get Educated:** If this is your first time using the Scrum methodology, do not attempt it without first getting yourself and the team educated on Scrum. While a lot of Scrum is about commons sense project management, there is a vast body of Scrum knowledge that diverges significantly from traditional project management theories. Equipping everyone on the team with that knowledge is the first step in putting Scrum into action successfully

- **Get The Right Sponsor:** Since Scrum is "different" from most traditional PM methodologies, there are likely to be more people within the organization who oppose its adoption. However, if the project is well sponsored, especially by someone that is high up in the organization hierarchy, or who has good "street credibility" amongst rank and file employees, your chances of successfully putting Scrum in action dramatically improve

- **Attack Low-hanging Fruit First:** Rather than tackling the most difficult and challenging project first, use a few relatively simple and "doable" projects as Scrum test cases. Not only will this approach give your team the in-field experience needed to tackle more complex projects later, but it will also show Scrum skeptics that the methodology truly works

- **Be Realistic:** Forecasting is always a tricky business when it comes to real-life scenarios. Most new Scrum practitioners are overzealous and, in their eagerness to show how fast Scrum can deliver, underestimate delivery timelines. It is always good practice to add some (not a lot!) extra "runway" to your forecasts to make them realistic

- **Co-locate Teams:** Where possible, co-locate the Scrum team within premises. That's not always possible, and success can still be achieved with disparately located teams. However, healthy team dynamics is more easily fostered when colleagues work in close proximity to each other. Coordination and communication is also better achieved with co-located teams

- **Start Low-tech:** There is absolutely no need for you to rush out and spend thousands of dollars initially to acquire Scrum project management software. For novice Scrum adopters, and also where the scope of the project isn't expected to be overly complex, using home-grown tools like Excel is good enough. Ideally, even savvy Scrum professionals will recommend the use of old-fashioned Whiteboards and Sticky Notes to manage and track Scrum Backlogs and Events

- **Celebrate Success:** One of the most important ways that one can put the Maslow theory into action is by celebrating team success. Individual's need for Esteem and Self-Actualization can be greatly fueled when they receive praise, accolades and recognition before their peers for their contributions. That's what will go furthest in cementing an efficient team

3.2.1 Tweaking The Tips

Putting Scrum into action isn't an "all or nothing" proposition. The tips provided above are meant to serve as broad guidelines for putting Scrum into action quickly and efficiently. However, one should realize that individual organizational restrictions will hamper the adoption of some of those tips in their entirety. In such cases, adapt, tweak and bend them until they fit your individual needs.

For instance, investment in education is one of the most significant decisions that an organization preparing to adopt Scrum will have to make. And Scrum training isn't cheap (although it is worth every dollar spent!). In case of budgetary constraints, pay to train a single individual, who then comes back and trains the other team members.

Similarly, if it is too expensive to have the team co-located, invest in telecommuting, tele-presence and collaboration technologies that can put teams into "virtual co-location" instead.

4.0 LIVING SCRUM - THE USER STORIES

One of the most difficult challenges that Scrum Masters (and Product Owners) are likely to face is in defining exactly what the user wants the project to deliver. The challenge is even more pronounced in Scrum because each iteration (Sprint) is expected to end with the delivery of pieces of those requirements. So, if one doesn't get it quite right, even the very first Sprint might end up producing "unusable product"!

Luckily, Sprint has a very powerful tool to help practitioners define these requirements in great degree of detail. The tool is called the User Story.

4.1 What Is a User Story?

Simply put, a User Story is nothing more than a Use Case that illustrates the need for, and usefulness of, a specific feature or functionality of the product (be it a Software, Building or Aeroplane). As its name implies, User Stories are driven by the end-user, but their creation should be facilitated (moderated) by the Scrum Product Owner.

Over a course of several brainstorming sessions, the Scrum Team, Scrum Master and Product Owner work collectively with users to hammer out an exhaustive set of User Stories that define the product in its entirety. Once all of the User Stories are compiled, they can then be passed on to other Team roles (Designer, Architect, Coder, Tester) for subsequent transformational activity.

Scrum User Stories may equate to the Requirement Definition phase of a typical Waterfall managed project. However, unlike the Requirements Definition Document (RDD), which is frozen upon completion of the requirements gathering phase, User Stories are not "static" documents. They may change and evolve throughout the life of a Scrum project.

The hallmark of Scrum projects (and why they differ so dramatically from Waterfall) is that the methodology allows Scrum teams to adapt quickly to changing User Stories and accommodate changes in subsequent Sprints instead of pushing them into a new project. Successfully managing User Stories is very much part of how success of the Scrum project will be assured.

4.2 Structure Of User Stories

There are various forms that a User Story may take, but the most basic structure is something like this:

- As an {Actor}
    - I {want, or must, or any other Action}
        - So that {I can, or I am able to, or any other Achievement}

As you can see, documenting user needs in this "3-A" hierarchy (of Actor, Action and Achievement) offers the Scrum team great insight into what the user wants, why he/she needs it, and what he/she hopes to accomplish by asking for that particular feature/function. User Stories are an effective way to document the "Who?", "What?" and "Why?" of product requirements.

In the above format:

- **"Actor"** is the owner of the User Story, and refers to role or group that is requesting the Story. User Story best practices suggest that the role of the "Actor" should be defined in as much specificity as possible, such as "Sales Manager", "Product Manager", "Service Engineer", "Customer". This provides greater insight and context to the User Story than by simply saying *"I want the product to do such and such..."*

- **"Action"** defines the characteristic that the product should display. For instance, if it is a mandatory feature, use the prefix "must" (as in *'I must be able to...'*); and if the requirement is optional, use "want" (as in *"I want to be able to..."*)
- **"Achievement"** is the end accomplishment that the Actor desires from performing the "Action".

1   User stories

1.1 Time registration portal

Actors:	Project manager: The person that is responsible for the project Project member: A person working on the project

1.1.1 As a Project manager

User story ID	I want to...	so that...
1.	Add project members to my project	the project members can register hours on the project
2.	View report on total hours spent on the project	I can track the project and see if we are on budget

1.1.2 As a Project member

User story ID	I want to...	so that...
3.	Register hours on a project	my project manager know how much time I have spent on the project
4.	View a weekly report on total hours spent	I can see how much I have been working

SOURCE: BreathingTech.Com

4.3 Creating User Stories

So how does one go about creating good User Stories, and what are some of the characteristics of the process of producing valuable stories?

In August 2003, Agile expert Bill Wake coined the INVEST acronym to define what good User Stories are all about:

- **I** – Independent: They are separate (and separable) and not overlapping each other
- **N** – Negotiable: They are produced as a result of negotiated agreements between users and the Scrum Team
- **V** – Valuable: User Stories that don't deliver value to the "Actor" are of no use. Each User Story that goes into the Product Backlog must add value to the product, otherwise developing it will be a waste of resources
- **E** – Estimable: The User Story should be so defined, that it can be prioritized, ranked and (time) estimated (from a development and implementation view)
- **S** – Small: Keep stories small so that the end deliverable can be produced within the timeframe of the Sprint (1 to 4 weeks). If a story gets too big (or complex), it should be broken down into components, and potentially delivered over several Sprints
- **T** – Testable: User Stories should be framed in a way that they convey exactly what's wanted, and consequently developers can write appropriate test scenarios to ensure they validate what they have produced (see Acceptance Criteria below)

4.4 Acceptance Criteria

For each User Story produced, the Scrum Team must have corresponding Acceptance Criteria agreed by the Product Owner prior to estimating or scheduling its deliverable. Without developers knowing what users will accept (or reject), it is extremely difficult to estimate what's required (in terms of activity) to build the PBI, or how much time it will require to complete.

Good acceptance criteria must include:

- **Functional criteria:** These must define acceptable functionality (e.g. *"Pressing the start button should cause the engine light to turn on"* or "Clicking 'Send' should move the message to the out queue")
- **Non-functional Criteria:** These should highlight acceptable non-functional traits/characteristics (e.g. *"All 'Send' buttons must be grey and indented"*)
- **Outstanding Defects:** Each User Story must clearly outline what "minimum" standards the product must have in order to be put into service. It should also clearly define what will be acceptable as an "Outstanding defect" that can be scheduled and fixed later (in the next Sprint or subsequent Sprints).
- **Performance criteria:** Having testable User Stories is therefore a pre-requisite to building successful Acceptance Criteria. For instance, a User Story that says a piece of software should deliver

"acceptable response time" is not something that can be tested. One that says "a 5 second response time is required", on the other hand, can easily be validated during acceptance testing.

4.5 Managing User Stories

At the start of the project, all accepted User Stories form the entire universe of Product Backlog Items (PBIs). The Scrum Master, Product Owner and Scrum Team, in collaboration with other stakeholders (Users, Customers etc.) can jointly rank and prioritize each story in terms of urgency of need.

At each Sprint Planning meeting, a subset of the Product Backlog is reviewed for possible inclusion into the Sprint Backlog. User Stories that have either been successfully completed, or are in progress (included in the current Sprint) should be clearly indicated so as to provide an accurate picture of Product Backlogs.

The Sprint Backlog (representing effort on User Stories in progress) must be reviewed at the Daily Scrum Meeting, with updates made to it collectively by all present (Scrum Master, Product Owner, Scrum Team, Users, Customers etc.). This will provide all stakeholders an updated snapshot of the status of currently in-progress User Stories.

During a Sprint, if the Product Owner rejects the work done on a particular User Story, it should be removed from the Sprint Backlog and re-introduced into the Product Backlog.

Unless otherwise agreed by all concerned, such User Stories should normally be re-prioritized for inclusion in the upcoming Sprint.

Since User Stories are meant to be a "living" entity, the process of managing them is one of consultation and collaboration. Depending on how a project environment looks like prior to the next Sprint, a User Story that was scheduled for Sprint#5 could very well find itself being reprioritized and rescheduled for the upcoming Sprint (#2). That could be, for instance, as a result of users having implemented all Stories from Sprint#1, and realizing that implementation of this particular User Story needs to be expedited.

5.0 WHY SCRUM?

Using any tried and tested project management framework to run projects can yield significant benefits across the organization. Beneficiaries can include:

- Senior management
- Rank-and-file employees
- Customers
- Project Managers
- Developers
- Product Managers...and more

However, using Scrum provides benefits that conventional PM methodologies (like Waterfall) might potentially not offer, including:

- An increase to the organizations Return On Investment (ROI) by producing a steady and continuous set of value-added benefits (through successive Sprints) instead of delivering a waterfall of all benefits at the end of a project

- Since all stakeholders are continually and constantly engaged with the project, through successful Sprints (Iterations), the outcome is more reliable than one that engages with stakeholders at the start (Requirements gathering) and end (Acceptance testing)

- Overall project risk and uncertainty is dramatically reduced as a result of breaking down the deliverables into smaller, almost self-contained, Sprints

- By producing "deliverable product" at the end of short Sprints, the organization's "Time to market" is dramatically increased, because users don't have to wait until the product is fully "done" before implementing it

- A well organized Scrum Team is a lean and efficient work group that delivers productivity, creativity and innovativeness to the organization - more so than the top-down hierarchical team structures employed by conventional PM methodologies

The end result of using Scrum is that everyone across the organization benefits, not just the development team.

5.1 Setting Expectations

Although Scrum can be a powerful tool for expediting projects across the organization, Scrum sponsors should not expect it to be an overnight success. For instance, in organizations that have an entrenched culture of "hierarchy", and a deep-rooted distrust for new things, adopting Scrum might be more difficult a challenge to conquer. Scrum veterans therefore always counsel potential Scrum adopters to carefully manage organizational expectations before proposing the use of Scrum.

6.0 PROFESSIONAL SCRUM

As was noted in a previous section of this book, getting educated about various aspects of Scrum is a good way to ensure your Scrum projects end in success. However, not every team member might be interested in pursuing certification-level Scrum training. For them, perhaps attending one or two-day Scrum appreciation workshops or seminars may be a good starting point.

For those team members that are interested in going further with their Scrum training, there are a number of certification options available as proposed by the Scrum Alliance. Here are a few to consider:

SOURCE: Scrum Alliance.Org

6.1 Certified ScrumMaster® (CSM)

A Certified ScrumMaster® serves as a vital resource to help Scrum teams make proper use of Scrum, thereby enhancing the chances of a project's success. As a CSM, you will gain a deep understanding of Scrum values and practices, and their application, and will provide the Scrum team expertise and knowledge that typical PMs don't usually have.

As a CSMs, you will learn how to act as a "servant leader", which empowers you to lead the team without formal authority over them. You will also master the principles of the Scrum framework, and learn how to help the team navigate them. Most importantly, you will gain valuable skills on how to insulate the Scrum team from internal and external distractions which often serve to derail Scrum projects.

6.2 Certified Scrum Product Owner® (CSPO)

The Product Owner role is a pivotal position in the broader Scrum Team. As a CSPO, you will acquire in-depth knowledge of all necessary terminology, principles and practices that will allow you to successfully fulfil your responsibilities as a Scrum Product Owner. As noted earlier in the book, Product Owners wear dual hats - that of a conventional Product Manager as well as a Project Manager. As such, the CSPO designation will be of immense value to anyone desirous of stepping into that challenging role.

6.3 Certified Scrum Developer® (CSD)

Scrum product development is unlike the traditional Waterfall phased-project cycle approach. The CSD course will provide developers all the knowledge to sharpen their Agile development skills. In addition, developers will also master the science behind incremental development as advocated by Scrum, instead of a delivery at end-of-project lifecycle approach.

CSD have an edge over non-Scrum colleagues in that they not only learn Agile engineering, but are also exposed to the basic principles and practices of the Scrum framework.

6.4 Certified Scrum Professional® (CSP)

Certified Scrum Professionals (CSPs) are in-practice CSMs, CSPOs or CSDs that wish to take their Scrum certification to the next level. Every project delivery methodology can be stretched to its limits, and that's when organizations see additional benefits. This training will enable you to acquire additional skills and knowledge to help you challenge your Scrum Teams to extend their current boundaries of Scrum practice.

6.5 Certified Scrum Trainer® (CST)

When Scrum practice has made you perfect in the science of Scrum, it's time to learn the art of teaching Scrum. As a CST, you'll learn everything there is to know about translating your wealth of Scrum knowledge and experience, and passing it on to others.

Every organization that's committed to Scrum should consider having at least one CST on board. CST's will not only help Scrum practitioners in the organization keep their skills current, through continuous training, but could also wear the hat of Scrum Master or Product Owner, if required.

6.6 Certified Scrum Coach® (CSC)

For CSP's that wish to elevate their Scrum credentials, CSC might be the answer. As a CSC, you must be able to demonstrate that you have all the practical and theoretical knowledge of Scrum to qualify as a Coach to others - individuals, groups and organizations.

One pre-requisite to attaining the CSC designation is that you must be able to prove that you have helped at least one organization successfully adopt Scrum in the implementation of real-life projects.

7.0 CONCLUSION

As the world of business grew more competitive, project sponsors were looking for a way to hasten the delivery of projects so they could get a competitive edge through faster time-to market. Project Management specialists came up with the Agile framework to support that goal. Scrum is one such Agile methodology that differs from traditional Waterfall approaches, in that it delivers product in incremental cycles called Sprints.

The entire universe of product features is managed in a Product Backlog, which is then broken down into smaller backlog items through a Sprint Backlog. Sprints are usually development cycles of no more than 1 month duration. During the life of a Sprint, each workday starts with a 15-minute stand up meeting called the Daily Scrum Meeting.

These are pulse-taking sessions that help manage the project through the Sprint lifecycle.

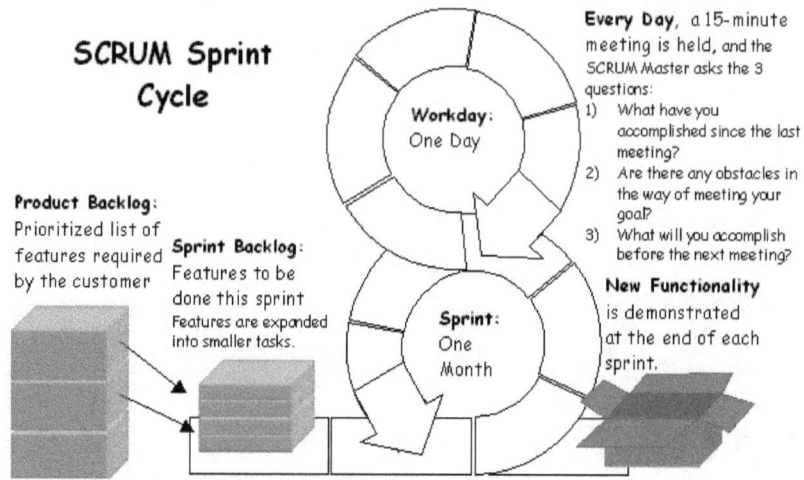

SOURCE: Revampologist.files.wordpress.com

Scrum proposes an "inspect and improve" methodology to make sure better project management practices are introduced if anything is found lacking. These best practice introductions are possible both at the end of each Sprint in the Sprint Review, as well as the Sprint Retrospective session. To be successful, Sprint Teams must adopt certain Rules and Norms, and project activity must be conducted through role-based Events that are "managed" by Scrum Masters, Product Owners and self-driven Scrum Teams.

One of the main hallmarks of Scrum Teams is that they are self-driven, self-managed entities, which means they are not organized in the typical Waterfall-driven top-down team hierarchy. Scrum Masters would therefore be wise to learn the psychology of "leading without authority" in order to get the group to work towards common goals.

Scrum project success also hinges on making sure the teams have a good balance of skill sets required for the project, and are backed by an adequate level of sponsorship. Teams are best if they are small in size - between 5 to 8 members. However, additional expertise may be brought to bear by engaging "limited duration" Subject Matter Experts (SMEs) as and when required.

Success will be greatly assured if everyone involved in a Scrum project is trained and educated in the basic Scrum philosophy, with more specific training provided to key players, including Scrum Masters, Product Owners and Developers.

Often, when new methodologies are being adopted, the temptation is to go in with a "big bang". Resist that temptation at all cost! Rather, adopt Scrum for smaller projects first, and upon wetting your feet in its ocean of knowledge, you can take the BIG PLUNGE.

Also, don't be in any hurry to spend too much money on automated tools. Where possible, try out free version of those tools first, or simply stick to less costly alternates (spreadsheets, white boards and sticky notes) to manage Scrum projects initially.

8.0 USEFUL RESOURCES

Here is a list of resources that Scrum practitioners and aspiring Scrum adherents may find useful. Some of these are informational in nature, and will help provide you greater insight into the Scrum world. Others are links to tools that you might find useful as you plan or implement Scrum throughout your organization.

It is important to keep in mind that these are not product or tool recommendations by the author. They are simply a collection of resources that you can leverage to conduct your own research on suitability (or otherwise) for your Scrum efforts.

Some of these tools have "FREE" versions that you might consider using as evaluation options.

Useful Scrum Product/Tool Links
Scrum software tools: http://www.scrumdesk.com/
Scrum software tools: http://www.axosoft.com/
Scrum software tools: http://www.collab.net/products/scrumworks
Tele-presence: AT&T Tele-presence solutions
Tele- presence: Cisco Tele-presence solutions
Collaboration solutions: Ormuco Communications
Virtual presence solutions: Polycom video collaboration solutions
Storyboard tools (for User Stories): http://www.storyboardthat.com/
Storyboard tools (for User Stories): http://storiesonboard.com/
Product/Sprint Backlog and Taskboard management tools: http://www.tinypm.com/
Backlog and Task management tools: http://agilefant.com/